Games and Rhymes
for Dog Training Times

Games and Rhymes for Dog Training Times

EXERCISES by Allan Bauman CPDT

ILLUSTRATIONS by Mike Ayers

The Wooster Book Company
Wooster Ohio ❁ 2006

The Wooster Book Company
where minds and imaginations meet
205 West Liberty Street
Wooster, Ohio ❀ 44691

ISBN 10: 1-59098-468-4
ISBN 13: 978-1-59098-468-0

∞ This book is printed on acid-free paper.

Dedication

First and foremost, I Dedicate this book to the Lord. He played a very important role in the development of this book. He helped me to understand and appreciate the value of relationships. I have been blessed with a wonderful family and have had the opportunity of experiencing our children develop a bond with our family dogs.

This book is dedicated to relationships. As you work with each of the exercises, I hope they help to develop a family bond and bring you memories to last a lifetime.

A Special Thank You to Derek and Tammy Dekens and the staff at Sit Happens. They truly gave me a special opportunity to work and test the exercises with children of all ages and with many breeds of dogs.

And Thanks to Kurt Knebusch for his editorial assistance and to Mike Ayers for his delightful drawings of the children and dogs in this book.

And a Very Special Thank You to The Wooster Book Company who brought so many aspects of this project together. Without their expertise and talent, this book would not have been possible. It has been great fun working together on this project.

—*Allan*

Introduction

I'm sure you remember good ol' Shep. Spot. Skippy. Mindy. The name is unimportant. The dog was your dog or a neighbor's dog. It was so smart it didn't need training. The dog, it seemed, knew everything.

Those are fond memories, I bet. Remembering a girl and her puppy. A boy and his dog. Summer. Fun. The good old days.

This book incorporates favorite games and nursery rhymes, ones likely known by you and your child, into a special type of dog training—training that creates a close bond between your child and his or her dog. The aim is for your child to gain fond memories like you have of Shep.

The exercises are designed to be simple, allowing the child and the dog to develop together. Both will be encouraged, not discouraged, as they go. A close bond will grow in the process.

As your child and your pet develop, you can also use these exercises for higher-level training. I've used them myself in a different format for advanced, sophisticated training. My challenge here was to create a book that a child will easily understand.

—Allan Bauman

Foreword

The idea of this book is to help you implement simple dog training games with your child. The goal is for your child to forge a deep, strong friendship with his or her dog and to have a dog that listens to and respects your child, leading to a relationship in which the child and dog can play together with good manners toward each other.

The instructions are short, simple, and clear. Helpful pictures accompany them. Your child can read the words as well as follow the pictures to know what to do. In the back of the book you'll find further explanation of the uses and purpose of the exercises.

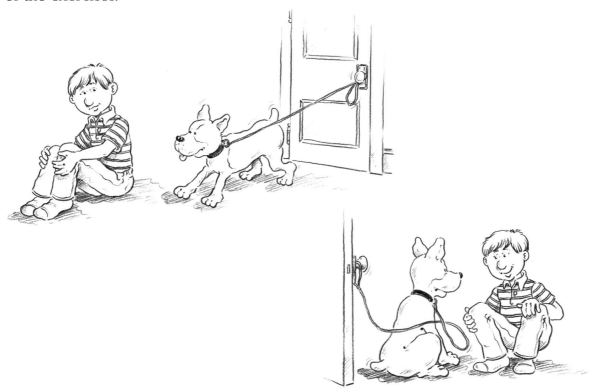

What we mean by "restraining your dog"

Attach the dog's lead to a sturdy stationary object such as a doorknob, a heavy chair, or a basement post. This lets the child step out of reach of the dog.

Young Maddie Hubbard

Young Maddie Hubbard
Went to the cupboard
To get her gold doggie a treat.
And when it did sit
She said to "Take it"
And so the gold doggie did eat.

Let's go to the cupboard and get our dog a treat! This is a way to teach your dog to take a treat politely.

1. Start with your dog sitting.
2. Reach into the treat container. Make sure the dog remains sitting.
3. If the dog moves or fidgets, move the treat away.
4. When the dog sits still, offer him the treat again.
5. The dog must take treat gently.
6. Move the treat away if the dog takes it roughly.
7. Say, "Take it" and give the dog the treat.

Howdy Puppy

Say, friends, what time is it?
It's howdy puppy time!
It's howdy puppy time!
It's howdy puppy time!
Me and my dog Drew
Say "Howdy pup!" to you!
Let's give a canine cheer,
because my puppy's here!

Dogs get excited when greeting children. Often we try to pet them
to calm them. Instead it's much better to wait for the dog to become calm
before we pet her or give her attention.

1. Restrain the dog.

2. Wait until the dog sits or lies down.

3. Step toward dog to pet her.

4. If the dog moves, step away from her.

5. Repeat steps 2–4 until the dog stays still.

6. Give the dog a treat.

7. Pet the dog for thirty seconds (count the seconds: "one alligator,
   two alligator …")

8. Step away.

9. Repeat steps 2–7 five or six times.

Knick, Knack, Scratchy Scratch

This young pup has an itchy belly—
An itchy belly and it shakes like jelly!
With a knick, knack, scratchy scratch,
Give the pup a bone,
Then call Grandma on the phone!

Give your dog a bone! And while you're at it, learn gentle petting and handling skills.

1. Let your dog nibble or lick a soft treat.
2. Pet or scratch different parts of your dog.
3. If the dog moves, stop treating and petting him.
4. When the dog is still, try again.
5. Pet and scratch different areas before giving a treat.

Eeny, Meeny, Miney, Moe

Eeny, meeny, miney, moe!
Treat your puppy, ho ho ho!
If she's good then tell her so!
Eeny, meeny, miney, moe!

Your mother says pick the very best one! In this game you choose which treat or reward your dog gets.

1. Place a treat on the floor. Make sure the dog doesn't sneak it!
2. Place another treat two feet away from the first one.
3. Point to the treats and say "Eeny, Meeny, Miney, Moe."
4. Choose one of the treats to give your dog.
5. Point to it and say "Take It."
6. If the dog tries to sneak the treat, quickly pick the treat up and start over.
7. Try adding more treats.

Eat Your Spinach

I'm puppy, the steak-bone fan!
I'm puppy, the steak-bone fan!
I'm strong to the finich,
I also eat spinach—
(and cheese!)
(and even my stinky medicine!)
I'm puppy, the steak-bone fan!

We can't eat candy all the time. Nor can dogs eat their favorite treat
  all the time. This game will help you choose the reward you give your dog.

1. Get two different treats that you know your dog likes.

2. Give the dog its second-favorite treat first.

3. As soon as the dog eats that treat, give her the first favorite treat.

4. Repeat steps 2 and 3.

5. Continue steps 2 and 3, changing to treats your dog may not like as well.

6. When changing treats, make sure your dog eats the treat you give her.

Shoo, Pup

Shoo, pup, don't bother me!
Shoo, pup, don't bother me!
Shoo, pup, don't bother me!
'Cuz now I need to studee-ee!

There will be times you don't want your dog to bother you. This exercise
will teach your dog to lie quietly at those times.

1. Restrain your dog.

2. Start with the **Howdy Puppy** game.

3. Pet or play with the dog.

4. Say "That's enough!" and step back so the dog can't reach you.

5. Wait for the dog to lie down.

6. Throw a treat far enough away that the dog has to get up to get it.

7. Wait for the dog to lie down again.

8. Repeat steps 6 and 7 until the dog lies down quickly.

Simon Says

Simon says "Sit!"
Simon says "Down!"
Simon says "Shake,
and shake it all around!"

Puppy gets a bone,
Puppy gets a treat,
If Simon says "Sit!"
And she takes her seat!

There are two simple rules to this game. First, your dog must listen
to what you say in order to get a treat. And second, make sure your dog
responds after only one request– "Sit" –not after repeated requests
("Sit … Sit … *Sit!*").

1. Start by restraining your dog so it's just out of your reach (as at the start
   of **Howdy Puppy** and **Shoo, Pup**).
2. Ask your dog to do an exercise, like *Sit* or *Down*. If the dog listens to you
   and does what you ask, give her a treat.
3. If the dog doesn't listen or do what you ask, then turn away and
   count to five.
4. If the dog is quiet and watches you, ask the dog to do the exercise again.
   If she does, then give her the treat.

Ring Around the Billy

Ring around my doggy Bill
Making sure that he stays still.
Pet him! Pet him!
Must–stay–down!

Children and dogs love to frolic. Teach your dog proper manners when playing, even if he gets excited.

1. The dog should know **Shoo, Pup** and be restrained if necessary.
2. Start to play with your dog.
3. If your dog jumps or nips, these are bad manners.
4. Step away from the dog so he can't reach you.
5. Wait until the dog lies down before you play with him again.
6. Repeat steps 2–5 until your dog plays with good manners.

Pop Goes the Puppy

Round and 'round the treat-snacks box
The monkey chased the puppy.
The monkey thought 'twas all in fun–
Pop! goes the puppy!

In this exercise, you'll teach the dog to do what you tell her to do—*Sit, Lay,* or *Down,* for example—until you say she can stop.

1. Place a treat on the floor.
2. Watch that the dog doesn't try to sneak the treat. Make sure you can get to the treat before the dog does, in case it does try to sneak it.
3. Walk around the dog, around the room, or around the treat. Make sure the dog doesn't try to sneak the treat.
4. When you're ready, give your dog the *Pop* command and let him get the treat.

Red Light, Green Light

Red light, stop!
Green light, go!
Eat the treats
you find in a row!

In this game, you get to be the traffic cop and tell the dog to stop or go.

1. Have the dog sit in front of you.

2. Take four steps backward with the dog following you.

3. You're the Traffic Cop. Raise your hand and say "Stop."

4. When the dog stops, drop a treat and say "Go."

5. Now have your dog *Sit.*

6. Walk backward about six or eight feet away from the dog.

7. Place four or five treats two feet apart in a row as you walk backward.

8. Stop your dog at each treat before you say "Go."

9. If your dog runs the "Stop" sign, put your foot over the treat before she gets to it.

Catch Me If You Can

Go get Stan and also Jan and a
pan and a fan and a van that is tan.
It's time to laugh and chase me, man,
It's time to Catch Me If You Can.

Can you run away from your dog? In this exercise, each time your dog catches you, you have to give him a reward—or, instead, just pet him.

1. Walk four or five steps away from your dog.
2. When your dog catches up to you, give him a reward.
3. Move away faster.
4. Reward your dog when he catches you.
5. Throw a treat.
6. When your dog goes for the treat, move away from him.
7. When your dog catches you again, give him another reward.
8. Move away farther and faster, rewarding him each time he catches you.

Red Rover, Red Rover

Red Rover! Red Rover!
Let Rover come over!
Run past the stuff that's in your way,
And come to me so we can play!

Let's see how many things your dog will come through to get to you!

1. Have an adult hold the dog while you walk away from her.

2. Encourage your dog to come.

3. The adult releases the dog to you.

4. Reward the dog when she reaches you and sits.

Further Fun:

1. Have an adult tie a string to a toy or a bone.

2. The object is placed between the adult and the child, but not on the dog's straight path to the child.

3. The child calls the dog.

4. If the dog veers from coming to the child, use the string to pull the treat away from the dog.

5. When the dog reaches the child, the child can either give a treat or take the dog to the object and untie the string, giving the dog that treat.

Hup, Two, Three, Four

Hup, two, three, four,
All you puppies on the floor!
Five, six, seven, eight,
March around and don't be late!

Ever like to march around? This is a wonderful exercise to train
   your dog to pay attention and march with you.

1. Using a treat, guide the dog to your left side.
2. Have the dog sit straight at your side.
3. Show the dog a treat, then march one step. *Hup!*
4. Stop and treat the dog.
5. Repeat step 1 four or five times.
6. See how far you can march between giving treats.

Remember that when you're marching, both you and your dog should
   keep in step. March as if you're in a parade!

Chug-a-tug, Spot!
Chug-a-tug, Blinky!
Chug-a-tug, pups, till you get real stinky!
Drop the tug when I say "Please,"
And I will give you cheddar cheese!

Dogs love to grab toys and play tug-of-war for attention. You want to teach them that there are only certain toys they can play tug with and that they should give up a toy when requested. This game helps you do that.

1. Get an appropriate tug-of-war toy, and get the dog to play tug.
2. Tell the dog to "Let go!"
3. If the dog lets go, give her a treat, and start to play the game again.
4. If the dog hangs on, then *you* let go.
5. Turn your back to the dog until it brings the toy back to you and drops it.
6. Don't try to grab the toy from the dog.
7. When the dog drops the toy, give her a treat and play again.
8. Give rewards and do the exercise again until the dog releases the tug right away when you ask for it.

Take Puppy Out to the Ballgame

Take puppy out to a ballfield
Put puppy out on the mound,
Give her some dog bones and rawhide chews,
I don't care if we win or we lose.
For it's root, root, root for my puppy
She loves me calling her name.
For it's one, two, three treats
She gets at the old ballgame!

To play this game, your dog should know **Red Light, Green Light.**

It's easier to start this game with a parent or other adult on first and third base.

1. Stand at home plate.
2. The dog is on the pitcher's mound.
3. Throw a treat to first or third base.
4. If the dog stays, point to the treat and say "Take it."
5. If the dog moves, the adult at the base picks up the treat.
6. Next, throw a treat to each base while the dog waits for the *Take it* command
7. Point to either base and say "Take it."
8. Try this exercise without adults at the bases.

Kids spend lots of time playing on the floor. This game is designed
to teach your dog how to behave around sleeping children or
children who are lying on the floor playing.

1. Restrain the dog and wait until he lies down.
2. Make sure the dog can't reach you.
3. Lie down in front of the dog.
4. Color a picture or play with toys.
5. Give the dog occasional treats for lying quietly.
6. Now try this exercise in an area where the dog can reach you.
7. If the dog gets excited or moves, move away again.

Go to Sleep

Lullaby, and good night,
with a ham bone to bite!
With a blanky o'er spread
is my puppy's soft bed!

Young Maddie Hubbard

Frequently children will give their dog a treat for doing an exercise well. But they sometimes forget to make the dog behave *while* they're giving the treat. It's just as important to make sure the dog behaves *while* it's getting the treat. This little exercise sets the stage for many other exercises in this book. It all starts here.

Howdy Puppy

Dogs get excited when children approach. Frequently the child will pet the dog while it's excited, in an attempt to calm the dog. This simple exercise works very well to teach the dog to sit and to remain sitting on his own. Encourage the child to watch for even the slightest sign of movement. If the dog indeed moves, have the child remain out of reach, ignoring the dog, until he stays still while the child approaches. Remind the child to step away if the dog moves while he's being petted.

Knick, Knack, Scratchy Scratch

This is a two-fold exercise; it builds the dog's trust for being petted and handled by children and, just as important, it gives you the opportunity to teach your child proper petting and handling of the dog. You can start by taking a small disposable cup with peanut butter in it and allowing the dog to lick the peanut butter as the child pets the dog. Progress to the point where the dog will allow the child to pet and groom different areas before giving the reward. You can use a brush or a comb, for example, instead of petting by hand.

Eeny, Meeny, Miney, Moe

This exercise really builds a lot of reward and control. Dogs often lose focus when rewards are present. The dog will learn to focus on the child rather than on the reward. Through this exercise, the dog will advance very rapidly in following directions.

Eat Your Spinach

I'm sure you've experienced this with your dog. There is a treat or distraction that the dog finds much more interesting than what you are offering. This exercise will help eliminate this problem. The dog will learn to work for what you are offering even if she doesn't actually like the reward. Why? Because it could lead to a very special treat! By practicing this exercise, you may even train your dog to readily take her medicine in order to get that savory piece of cheese.

Shoo, Pup

It happens all the time. Dogs nudging, crawling into laps, pawing, and barking to get our attention. We are busy and the dog nudges us. We either pet the dog or focus our attention on the dog to get him to lie down. Either way, we've paid attention to the dog when he has bothered us. With this exercise, you will give the dog attention and then ignore him until he lies down. Your dog will learn to lie down and behave to get your attention.

Simon Says

How many times do you have to repeat "Sit, Sit, *Sit*" before you dog will Sit? In this exercise, we will teach the dog to perform on the first command or we quit the game and ignore him and don't give him a treat. Watch your child closely so that she gives the dog only one chance to listen. There are two simple rules to this game: First, your dog must listen to what you say in order to get a treat; and second, you must make sure your dog responds after just one request—**Sit**—not after repeated requests (Sit … Sit … *Sit!*). First, restrain the dog, then ask the dog to do an exercise like Sit or Down. If the dog listens to you and does what you ask, give her a treat. If the dog doesn't listen, turn away and count to ten. Then wait for the dog to look at you and ask again. Repeat the exercise until your dog obeys right away after you ask the first time.

Ring Around the Billy

It's best to restrain the dog in the beginning of this exercise so the child can step within reach of the dog. The child begins to play with the dog. Include games that may normally cause the dog to jump, nip, or become overly excited. If the dog displays any bad manners, the child simply steps out of reach of the dog. Repeat this activity until the dog quits using bad manners. This is an excellent exercise to train the dog to behave while children are playing. It helps to teach manners such as not to nip or jump up.

Pop Goes the Puppy

This is a great way to begin teaching the **Stay** exercise. The child starts by putting a treat on the floor, but make sure the child can get to the treat before the dog can, should the dog try to sneak the treat. The child begins with simple challenges by walking just two or three steps away. Make sure to reward the dog by periodically giving him the treat on the floor. The child can even try putting a treat on each of the dog's front paws, then standing up straight, counting to five, then telling the dog to eat the treats. The child can leave a treat on the floor and develop the exercise to the point of being able to walk out of the room!

Red Light, Green Light

When perfected, this is one of my favorite and most useful exercises. The child will be able to have the dog **Stop** and listen to commands from a distance. The child can also throw several treats on the floor in different areas and work at directing the dog to the treats, almost like a traffic cop directing traffic. If you develop this exercise, your dog will become very attentive and focused and will begin to follow directional hand signals. The exercise also works very well in helping teach the **Stay** exercises. Children should start off with a mild distraction and practice for short periods. As the dog succeeds, the child can make the game more challenging.

Catch Me If You Can

This is a great exercise to teach the dog to follow children or to walk with them. As the dog begins to keep up with the child, have the child walk in a straight line. Soon the dog will follow the child longer distances between treats. To really develop this exercise, when the dog and child are walking together in a straight line, the child can do the opposite of the dog if the dog leaves the child. For example, if the dog starts to walk faster, the child slows down. If the dog slows down, the child speeds up. If the dog goes to the left, the child goes to the right. Have your child watch the dog closely and change as soon as the dog stops following the leader.

Red Rover, Red Rover

This is a great exercise for teaching the dog to come when called. The most important part of this exercise is to set up the distractions so you can keep the dog from getting to them if the dog goes to the distractions rather than to the child. Here are some hints: tie a string to a bone, or perhaps have another family member try to entice the dog to come to them. Remember that if the dog goes to another person, that person must immediately hide her treat from the dog. Once the dog goes to the child that originally called the dog, the child can send the dog to another family member who has a treat. Just a reminder: the person who calls the dog is the only person who can give the treat. Try having different family members call the dog back and forth.

Hup, Two, Three, Four

This exercise trains the dog to walk precisely at the child's side. It is the advanced level of **Catch Me**. In **Catch Me**, the exercise teaches the dog to come to the child and to follow the child. In **Hup, Two, Three, Four**, the dog will still follow the child but the focus will be on having the dog keep up with the child. You'll find that the dog will soon get distracted. Try having the child march past hotdogs, biscuits, or other treats placed on the floor, then have the dog go back to get the treats. Adult assistance might be helpful in this exercise. Tie a string to a biscuit or position yourself so if the dog leaves the child for the treat, you can quickly pick up the treat.

Chug-a-Tug

It happens all the time: dogs take things they shouldn't have. **Chug-aTug** will teach your dog two important things: to give up things when requested, and what items she can play with. In the beginning, when taking an object from the dog, give the dog a treat and immediately give the object back. Repeat taking and treating five or six times and you will soon see the dog offering the object for the treat and losing interest in the object. Do this with any object, even an off-limits one such as a good shoe. Once the dog gives up objects readily, any time the dog brings you an object that is not hers, take that object and then point to an acceptable object and have her bring that to you before giving the treat. Your dog will soon begin to focus only on objects that are hers.

Take Puppy Out to the Ballgame

This game teaches many exercises. It teaches the dog to **Stay**, focuses the dog's attention, and teaches the dog directional hand signals. It is one of those games that can be taken to an advanced level. Whether this exercise is played outside in the backyard or inside your house, it can be fun for both dog and child. I like to start by having the dog **Sit**, then I throw a treat to one side of the dog about five feet away from him. Then I point to the treat and say **Take It**. I repeat this on the other side of the dog. If the dog is readily responding, I throw a treat to both sides of the dog. The dog usually looks at only one treat. Point to the other treat and if necessary, step toward the other treat until the dog looks at it. When the dog focuses on that treat, tell the dog to **Take It**, making sure he takes the one you pointed to. Develop this exercise until you can have the dog look back and forth to each of the treats before you say **Take It**.

Go to Sleep

All too often children will be relaxing or playing on the floor when in comes the dog bouncing all over them and their games. **Go to Sleep** teaches the dog to lie quietly when children are playing games or relaxing. Remember to start with the dog being restrained. The child should gradually move into the area within the dog's reach. If the dog gets excited, the child should move out of the dog's reach. Keep the dog restrained until the dog is reliable and the child can play quietly within the dog's reach before removing the restraint.

Allan Bauman, with grandchildren Ahna (left) and Madison (right),
giving Píli, a mixed-lab, a treat

Allan Bauman CPDT has been training dogs and instructing classes for over thirty years. He is known for his gentle and effective training methods. This book uses games and rhymes to help children successfully train their own dogs.

Allan is a charter member of the APDT (Association of Pet Dog Trainers). He has served on the APDT board, is a past president of the APDT, and has lectured both nationally and internationally.

Allan's *"Paw-sitive" Dog Training* program (book and video) has received favorable recognition. His DVD, *Children and Dogs*, is also available. To order, visit *www.dogwise.com* or *www.tawzerdogvideo.com*.